DANIELLE

CAREER PLANNING HANDBOOK

Navigating Your Future Career and Work Life

Published in 2024 by Amba Press, Melbourne, Australia
www.ambapress.com.au

© Danielle Flack 2024

All rights reserved. No part of this book may be reproduced or transmitted in any form or by any means, electronic or mechanical, including photocopying, recording or by any information storage and retrieval system, without prior permission in writing from the publisher.

Cover design: Tess McCabe
Internal design: Amba Press
Editor: Rica Dearman

ISBN: 9781923116399 (pbk)
ISBN: 9781923116405 (ebk)

A catalogue record for this book is available from the National Library of Australia.

Contents

Introduction: How did we think about careers in the past? 1

Chapter 1 Who am I? Unleashing your career potential 5

Chapter 2 Are you the main character in your career story? 13

Chapter 3 Exploring possibilities 19

Chapter 4 Use your brain to help you get ahead in your career 25

Chapter 5 Setting goals for future success 31

Chapter 6 Dream it and make it visual 35

Chapter 7 Take your dream for a test drive! 47

Chapter 8 Top tips and advice when considering study options 51

Chapter 9 Start building your skills and experience now! 57

Chapter 10 Reflect, evaluate and readjust 73

INTRODUCTION

How did we think about careers in the past?

How we think about the world of work (and jobs and careers) has changed dramatically over the past 70 years. Your grandparents' generation most likely worked in the same industry for their entire career life. It is likely that they started at the 'bottom' as a trainee or assistant and worked their way up through a company or organisation, learning skills and gaining experiences on the job.

It was common for people to enter the workforce straight from school (usually without completing Year 12), and only a small number of jobs required a university degree. Women in particular had very limited career options, with roles like nursing, teaching and secretarial work being their main source of employment. Even then, most women were forced to quit their jobs once they got married and started a family. Career advice was limited, and most people thought that the best way of determining career choice was by matching your personality with jobs or work environments that required specific personal attributes or characteristics.

But it wasn't long before people started to realise that choosing a career was more complicated than just working out what type of personality you have and then matching that to a job. Factors such as our past experiences and personal motivations began to influence career choice, as did an increasing awareness that our goals, interests and motivation to work can change throughout our life. And just as we change and grow throughout our lives, it became more acceptable for our career choices to grow and change, too! People began to consider how attributes like experience, learning and the development of new skills and knowledge can lead to new career goals.

Another major change in career advice happened when people began to think more about the things that limit our career choices. There was a growing awareness that not everyone has access to the same variety of career options. Factors such as gender, age, social status, family responsibilities and even access to education play an important role in determining the career options we have access to.

How do we think about careers now?

In today's society, people change jobs (and careers) more frequently. In fact, it is believed that young people today will have more jobs and unique career paths than any other generation in history. This might include changing employers, switching to a similar job in a different industry or changing your career completely. Sometimes these changes are by choice, for example, a person may choose to use the skills and experience they have developed as a nurse to gain employment in an organisation promoting healthcare initiatives. Or a lawyer may decide to put their knowledge of policy and ability to understand legislation to use working as a property developer.

Some jobs are disappearing...

Sometimes people are forced to change jobs because of limited employment opportunities or because their current job is no longer required. This might be because of advancements in technology or automation, or because of the rising costs of labour. This can happen when a job involves tasks that are repetitive, or they follow a set process like assembling a product. These types of jobs can be performed by a machine or robot at a cheaper cost, so there isn't a need to employ a human being to perform the task any more.

And sometimes jobs disappear because society has changed and the need for a particular job no longer exists. For example, before people had toilets inside their homes, most toilets were outside. There wasn't sewage and plumbing like we have today, so someone had to come and collect the waste, just like we get our bins emptied each week. Obviously, as technology and infrastructure developed, the need for weekly sewage collection decreased and the need for waste collectors also disappeared.

It's OK, though... new jobs are constantly emerging!

It's important to remember, though, that while some jobs are disappearing, new jobs are also being created. One area that is expanding rapidly is the field of digital technology. While jobs in digital technology are not new, the opportunities that exist now are more diverse than ever before.

In the past, when we thought about a job in IT, we probably thought it involved software development, coding, creating computer games or fixing computers. But as technology (and the internet) has moved away from being something only associated with a computer, and has truly become something that is embedded in our everyday lives, the need for employees who specialise in a range of areas within computer science, digital technology and even cybersecurity has grown and expanded. We now have jobs such as software architects,

UX specialists and even information security analysts that have emerged in response to our changing and developing relationship with technology.

Having high levels of digital literacy and the ability to use and adopt new and emerging technology is also no longer important just for those who have an IT qualification. More and more frequently, digital literacy is becoming a standard skill sought after by employers, and having a high level of digital literacy skills is seen as a common expectation for employees.

How do we 'keep up'?

The first step in planning for a world that is changing and a future that we can't predict involves embracing the uncertainty and acknowledging that we will have to be flexible, to adapt and to respond to change throughout our career life. We will have to learn new skills, adjust to new ways of doing things and engage in ongoing learning opportunities. We must also learn to become the managers of our own careers.

The reality is that we will change our jobs many times – and our jobs themselves will change. Because of this, we need to become skilful at identifying and describing our skills, knowledge and experience, understanding labour market information and identifying gaps in our knowledge. We will need to adopt a growth mindset, be flexible and adaptable, and recognise that learning will continue throughout our lives (and not end when we finish high school or even university).

I really hope this book inspires you to plan your future career with confidence and that you enjoy the process of doing so along the way.

CHAPTER 1

Who am I? Unleashing your career potential

At different points in your life, you will need to make career decisions. At school, this might look like picking subjects for Years 11 and 12 or thinking about post-school options like TAFE, university, work or an apprenticeship. Making good decisions involves career planning, but career planning is not always an easy task. Sometimes it feels like everyone in your life has advice, an idea or an opinion about what you should study or what career might suit you. While it is helpful to have a strong network of people around you who can support you on your career journey, sometimes all of these outside voices can leave you feeling more confused.

This is especially the case when these voices are saying things that contradict each other, or when the advice and suggestions that are being shared aren't aligned with your own ideas or aspirations. It can be difficult at times to escape all the outside noise and really focus on your own interests, values and strengths. But taking time to think about, and reflect on, who you are right now, where you are heading and what you need to do to get there is vital to successful career planning.

What's your story?

"Embrace self-awareness as your guiding light. Only by knowing yourself can you navigate the vast sea of career choices and find the one that brings you joy and success."

– Maya Angelou

Before you can start planning your future, you need to spend some time understanding your story. This means digging deep into who you are and what makes you tick. This process is called self-awareness and is best described as the ability to focus on yourself and think deeply about how your actions, thoughts and emotions influence your decision-making. Self-awareness is achieved through the process of self-discovery – a journey that involves learning about who you are, what you value and what you need (and want) out of life.

It may surprise you to learn that developing a strong sense of self-awareness is closely connected to the success of your future career journey.

There are three aspects to developing a strong sense of self-awareness. Understanding these is like having a compass that will help guide you towards a fulfilling and successful career. They are:

1. Finding your purpose
2. Identifying your passions
3. Understanding your perspective

Finding your purpose

Your purpose encompasses the guiding principles that define who you are and what you believe in. Your purpose is your motivation, your values, your driving force. It shapes your decisions, your actions and the way you interact with others.

People can be motivated by many things, such as financial success, personal growth, job satisfaction, a desire to help others or create a better world. People may value wealth, freedom, flexibility, creativity or even relationships with those around them.

When you are looking at purpose from the perspective of self-awareness, you need to think about your intrinsic motivation. Intrinsic motivation means being driven by the prospect of personal satisfaction or fulfilment. When you understand your purpose and your intrinsic motivation, you are able to take action from a place of joy and curiosity. You do things because you want to do them, not out of a sense of obligation, fear or expectation. This often means that you are more likely to follow things through, show greater commitment and be happier with your choices.

Purpose and career choice

Understanding your purpose can also help you identify the types of jobs, industries and careers you may like to explore in the future, and it may allow you to align your career choices with what truly matters to you.

It is important to remember that your purpose is not fixed. It is tied to your personality, your experiences and your priorities. As your experiences grow and change over time, you learn more about yourself and the world around you. This can mean that your preferences, your needs and wants can also change. All of these factors can influence your purpose.

Take action!

Spend 5-10 minutes thinking about your purpose.

- What motivates you to get out of bed in the morning?
- What do you value in life?
- What pushes you to work harder, overcome challenges or strive for more?

Identifying your passions

Your passions are the things in your life that you can't live without. They are the things that you invest time, energy and attention into – the activities that you enjoy doing, the tasks that bring you joy and excitement, and the things that spark your curiosity. Your passions push you to want to learn, grow and experience more.

Your passions can include interests both at school and in your home life. They can be subjects that you learn, activities that you enjoy doing or skills that you constantly want to develop and improve on.

The thing about passions, though, is that they aren't necessarily linked to aptitude or natural ability. We can be naturally good at things that we don't enjoy doing. This is because motivation often comes from challenges. If we don't feel challenged by something or feel as though we have to put in effort, we can get bored easily and lose interest.

Passions and career choice

Identifying your passions helps you to narrow down potential career options and allows you to focus your efforts into areas that align with your interests.

Sometimes talking about passions can make people feel uncomfortable. It can make them feel like they are being 'put in a box' or stereotyped. You might have lots of hobbies and things that you enjoy doing, for example, but nothing that you like doing enough to want to make a career out of. Afterall, just because you enjoy Maths, it doesn't mean that you will want to be an accountant when you finish school. Likewise, you might be a really talented artist or musician, but see this more as a hobby or something that you like to do for fun. It is important to remember that you can be interested in things and not want to make a job or career out of them!

Another reason people are reluctant to identify their passions is because they might not be able to see how their interests align with future career possibilities. You might have lots of interests and things that you enjoy doing, but not one thing that you are so passionate about that you can see yourself doing it for the rest of your life. On the other hand, you might not be able to see how all of the skills, experiences and knowledge that you are gaining may be leading you down a specific career path. You never know how your interests may come in handy in the future!

Enjoy the process

Rather than fixating on the outcome (for example, how you can turn your interests into a career), try focusing on the process. Think broadly and creatively about what you enjoy doing. Experiment and try out new things. Get curious about learning and don't worry if your passions change over time.

Take action!

Spend 5–10 minutes thinking about your passions. Remember, these could be things that you do at school or outside of school.

- What do you invest time, energy and attention into?
- What activities do you enjoy doing?
- What tasks bring you joy and excitement?
- What sparks your curiosity? What do you want to learn more about?
- What are your non-negotiables – the things that you can't live without?

Understanding your perspective

Your personal narrative is the story that you tell yourself about your life. It is important to invest time into thinking about your story because, after all, you are the expert of your life! The aim is to learn about your perspective on different things and understand what influences or shapes that perspective.

In order to understand your perspective effectively, there are three key principles that you need to keep in mind:

1. There is no 'objective reality' or absolute truth – just your perspective on things. What is true for you may not be true for someone else, or even for you at another point in time.

2. You construct your perspective through experiences and the interactions and conversations that you have with those around you. These experiences and interactions help you construct a personal narrative.

3. Language choices influence and reflect your interpretation and understanding of the world around you. This is demonstrated by the positive or negative ways that you talk to yourself (and about yourself) and to others, about your experiences, aspirations and challenges.

By reflecting on these key principles, you can gain a deeper understanding of yourself and develop a greater sense of control over your future career journey.

CHAPTER 2

Are you the main character in your career story?

How do you position yourself within your narrative? Do you turn to friends, family or teachers to tell you what to do, or are you a confident decision-maker? Are you easily influenced by what others suggest or are you committed to your own beliefs and values? These questions can help you to gain an understanding of how much agency you feel that you have. Agency refers to the level of control you feel over decision-making, your actions and their consequences.

Main character or supporting cast?

If you lack a sense of agency, it can feel like you are part of the supporting cast in your own life's story, as if things are happening to you and you can't stop or influence what happens. A lack of agency can lead to low self-confidence, causing you to procrastinate and feel indecisive. It can also cause you to actively avoid taking risks, even if they are small risks, with no long-term consequences.

Having a strong sense of agency means that you position yourself as the main character in your life's story. You feel empowered to set goals, explore options and take action. Having a strong sense of agency can also help you to advocate for yourself and your needs, and actually help you to feel like you are being heard.

Your feelings of agency are closely tied to your perspective and personal narrative. Consider the following example.

It is subject selection time at school, and you need to make decisions for your Year 11 and 12 program.

1. A student with low feelings of agency may tell themselves that they can't be trusted to make 'good' choices. They may seek advice from friends, family and teachers and begin to feel overwhelmed by the decision-making process. These students will often ask questions like: "What do you think I should do?" or "Can you just tell me what to pick?" They will be reluctant to make choices because they are fearful of getting it 'wrong'. They may start to procrastinate and avoid talking about their concerns. They will probably hand in their subject selection paperwork late – after picking the same subjects that their friends have picked because it was just easier to follow their lead.

2. A student with strong feelings of agency, on the other hand, will often embrace the chance to explore their options. They might talk to others and seek advice to gain extra information and clarity, not because they want (or need) someone else to make a decision for them. These students like to brainstorm and plan, but don't get caught up obsessing over minor details or things that they can't control. They understand that it is important to take action, and even if things don't work out as planned, they are prepared to reassess and realign their goals.

Which student are you? It's actually OK if you are the student who isn't feeling like they have a whole lot of agency at the moment! The first step of building a stronger sense of agency involves identifying your perspective on the world around you and thinking about the stories you tell yourself about your place in that world.

So, how do you do that? This involves examining your personal narrative and listening carefully to what you are telling yourself – about your abilities, your strengths and your desire to achieve future success.

Automatic thinking

In stressful situations or those where decisions need to be made, take time to pause and identify your automatic thoughts – these are the thoughts that pop into our head in different moments and influence how we feel or interpret a situation. They can also determine the way that we respond to that situation.

Negative thought cycles

Sometimes when we are operating from a space where we don't feel like we have a lot of control, we begin to be ruled by a cycle of negative automatic thinking. Examples of this type of thinking could be phrases like: "There's no point in trying because I'm never successful", "I don't have anything that I'm good at" or "Everyone else knows what they want to be when they finish school, but I don't have any idea".

In these types of situations, it is important to recognise this pattern of thinking and to identify the emotions or feelings that are contributing to it. They could be feelings of fear, sadness or worry – these are all very normal emotions. The point is not to stop these emotions from occurring, but to recognise why you are feeling this way.

Once we understand how thoughts are influencing our feelings, we can then start to exercise greater control over our response. A key to this involves questioning the assumptions that the negative automatic thoughts are based on, reframing the problem and shifting towards a willingness to explore an alternative perspective.

You can do this by running through the following checklist:

1. **Is my response based on emotions or facts?**

   Let's think about the phrase: "There's no point in trying because I'm never successful". What type of emotions might be behind this thought? There might be feelings of frustration that are the result of setbacks or challenges. There might be feelings of disappointment because you haven't been achieving the grades that you think you deserve. Or there might be a hint of jealousy that friends or peers seem to be achieving greater success than you are at the moment. These are all valid ways of feeling. But what are the facts? Let's turn the phrase on its head. When have you experienced success in the past? What do you enjoy doing? What do others say that you are good at?

2. **Is this a 'black or white' situation, or is there a grey area that I need to consider?**

   Sometimes we get stuck thinking about things in extremes. Things are either good or bad, right or wrong, and there isn't anything in between. This type of thinking seems to underpin a comment like: "I don't have anything that I'm good at". The suggestion here is that not being good at anything means that you are bad at everything – and this is highly unlikely! A major problem with this type of thinking is that it can prevent you from being open to exploration and growth. Rather than thinking that there isn't anything that you are good at, it can be helpful to instead think: "I haven't found the thing that I am really good at yet". This change in perspective encourages you to explore different possibilities and get curious about what you still have to learn and discover.

3. **What is the worst thing that could happen? Could I minimise the risk?**

    Making decisions is tough. Sometimes you make a great decision and things work out perfectly. But this isn't always the case. Many young people feel reluctant to make a decision about their future career journey because they think they need to know the 'right' answer and that if they don't make the 'right' choice, the consequences will be disastrous. So, when young people say things like: "Everyone else knows what they want to be when they finish school, but I don't have any idea", what they actually might mean is: "I feel like the consequences of making this decision are huge, there are so many options, and I'm scared to pick something in case it doesn't work out".

It's OK to change your mind

The good news is that when it comes to making decisions about subjects for Years 11 and 12, or even picking a course at university or TAFE, the consequences of a 'wrong' choice are rarely permanent and are hardly ever going to result in complete disaster. For example, if you pick a subject that you don't enjoy, it is often pretty easy to make a subject change at the end of a unit or semester. If you start a course that isn't what you expected, you can explore options to transfer to a different course in a similar area or a different course in a completely different area altogether.

Thinking about the worst thing that could happen usually helps you to realise that while there may be some minor inconvenience, it is usually easy to readjust your plans and explore an alternative pathway.

Take action!

Spend 5–10 minutes thinking about your personal narrative and your current perspective.

- What areas of your life do you currently feel like you don't have much control over? What is the source of these feelings?
- In situations where you need to make decisions, how do you respond? Do you feel confident or do you prefer for others to direct your decision-making? Why do you think that is?
- In stressful situations, what automatic thoughts pop into your head? Do these thoughts fit into the checklist above? If so, is there any way you can reframe the thoughts in a more positive or constructive way?

CHAPTER 3

Exploring possibilities

Once you have a clear understanding of your purpose, passions and perspective, it is important to start to consider the possibilities that exist. Self-awareness doesn't just mean understanding where you are right now, it also involves thinking about the person that you would like to become or the journey you'd like to take in the future.

While it is important to think about the future, it is also really important to recognise that the future is unknown and always changing. Therefore, the key to successfully thinking about future possibilities is being open-minded and open to change. This means considering multiple career pathways and a variety of possibilities.

The difference between a job and a career

Before you get too far into exploring possibilities, you need to consider the difference between a job and a career. A job is a specific role or position that a person undertakes for a wage (money!). When we refer to a career, we are talking more about a series of connected employment opportunities, where a person builds up skills and experience in a particular field over a longer period of time. It involves a progression of related jobs that offer growth, advancement and development.

In many ways, your career planning involves 'big-picture thinking' – the ability to dream, brainstorm ideas and explore multiple outcomes or possibilities. In this sense, your individual jobs are the stepping stones that you use to build your career. Each job that you undertake can help you to build and enhance your skills, knowledge and experience. This, in turn, allows you to progress to the next step in your career.

Career progression

It is important to remember that your career journey probably won't be linear. This means that it is unlikely to follow a straight path from point A to point B to point C. For many people, career progression looks more like a squiggly line.

This is because things don't always unfold in the way you expect them to. You might find yourself in a job where your opportunity to learn and grow is limited. You might find that what you thought was your dream job is actually really boring and repetitive. Likewise, you may get into a position that exposes you to experiences and opportunities that you had never previously considered, and this could change the direction of your career trajectory altogether!

Get comfortable with change

"Don't aim at success... the more you aim at it and make it a target, the more you are going to miss it. For success, like happiness, cannot be pursued; it must ensue..."

– Viktor Frankl

Why wouldn't you want to aim for success? Or happiness, for that matter? Because when you focus all of your attention on one thing, you can end up feeling disappointed and frustrated when things don't work out like planned. So, rather than focusing on a specific outcome, focus on the journey!

As the previous two chapters have shown, it is important to reflect on who you are right now before you can begin to make plans for the future. But part of this also involves recognising that who we are can and will change, as will the world in which we live. Trying to predict the future is very difficult, so we need to get comfortable with uncertainty and change.

Our identity is not fixed. Over time, as we engage in new experiences, interact with new people and learn new things, we continue to grow and change. Our interests change, our values change and our priorities change. This is OK and a perfectly normal thing that happens. It is for this reason that when it comes to thinking about career planning, you need to be flexible, adaptable and open to new opportunities and new possibilities as they emerge.

You will have numerous jobs

As you can see, career planning is not just about choosing a job and sticking with it until you reach retirement age – it is a lot more complicated than that! Research tells us that young people today will change their jobs, on average, every three and a half years. This means that if you start working when you are 18 years old and you retire when you are 70 (the predicted retirement age for young people today), you will have around 15 different jobs throughout your life. And these jobs will not all be within the same career area. Many people will change careers multiple times, too, using their transferable skills to gain employment across a range of different industries.

Learning from change

A common misconception is that we need to be successful in everything that we do and experience success the first time we do something. Not only does this idea create unnecessary pressure, but it is also unrealistic.

For example, let's talk about university study. Most young people think that at the end of Year 12, you pick a degree, you go to university for three or four years and then you start working in that field. For some people, this is the pathway that they follow. But for a lot of people, this isn't the case.

Firstly, not everyone who starts a degree at university completes that degree. Many students leave their course in the first year. Some return to study and change degrees, some defer and decide to travel or work and then return to study the next year or after an extended break. Some leave the degree altogether and do not return to university study, instead taking up an apprenticeship or traineeship, enrolling in TAFE or securing employment.

Find out how it worked for others

Talk to your family and friends and ask them about their experiences in the first few years after finishing high school and it is likely they will mention things like changing their minds, wanting to try new things and exploring different options.

You will also soon realise that most of these people have still experienced success even though their original plan didn't work out. In fact, most will probably talk about these setbacks or challenges as being beneficial learning experiences that helped them get to where they are today. This is because learning from mistakes and bouncing back after disappointment or setbacks is part of the journey!

Obviously, your career planning can't (and does not) stop when you leave high school and take a step into a course, training or employment. It is an ongoing process that requires you to develop goals, put in place a plan of attack, and then readjust and reassess as life unfolds. Developing a mindset that responds to change and setbacks in a positive way allows you to realign your career journey when things don't turn out as you plan, explore new possibilities and experience success.

CHAPTER 4

Use your brain to help you get ahead in your career

If someone tells you to use your brain to get ahead in your career, you might think that they are encouraging you to find a job that values your aptitude or intelligence. But they could also be encouraging you to use your brain's ability to change and grow to help you uncover new experiences and learn new skills.

Science has shown that our brain has an incredible power to change its activity and form new connections in response to learning opportunities and new experiences. This is referred to as neuroplasticity and basically means that your brain is malleable, or able to adapt and respond to stimulus.

While we used to think that the brain stopped forming quite early (once people became teenagers), we now know that our brains have the capacity to keep on changing and building new connections throughout our entire lives. A key aspect of this change relates to experiences. As we experience new things, we are teaching and re-teaching our brain how to respond. This is why taking action is so important! By trying things out, engaging in new experiences and learning new things, we are helping our brains to grow and develop.

Understanding the types of mindset

There is evidence to suggest that our attitude to learning and new experiences can also have an effect on our brain's neuroplasticity. This is referred to as our mindset. The easiest way to think about mindset is to consider your response and attitude to certain situations. It is the voice in your head telling you how to interpret the events that you experience. There are two types of mindset that relate to learning and personal development: fixed mindset and growth mindset.

To understand the difference, consider this example:

Imagine you receive a test back in your Maths class. Your result is lower than you were expecting. Here are two ways you could react:

1. You may get upset, refuse to read the feedback, and the negative automatic thoughts in your head tell you are not good at Maths and never will be, and that you should probably just stop trying. This may cause you to become disengaged in class or even try to change out of the subject altogether. These responses are reflective of a fixed mindset. Having a fixed mindset is based on the belief that your skills or ability to learn and improve is 'fixed' or stuck and therefore can't be changed, even if you invest time and effort. People who adopt a fixed mindset tend to avoid challenges and resist change because they fear failure.

2. Instead of getting upset when you get the test back and allowing negative automatic thoughts to influence how you respond, someone who adopts a growth mindset might recognise their disappointment and reflect on why they are feeling this way. Is it because you put in a lot of effort and you don't feel like the result reflects that? Is it because you care about your grades and want to do well? These are all reasonable responses and ways of feeling. But rather than seeing this setback as the end point, having a growth mindset involves viewing this experience as an opportunity to grow and develop further. This might mean taking time to read through the feedback provided by your teacher or organising a time to talk to them in person about your result and how you can improve in the future. Having a growth mindset means believing that you can learn and develop – even when you experience setbacks or challenges. It also involves taking action and responding to feedback, rather than sitting back and letting things happen to you.

How mindset influences career planning

The principles of fixed and growth mindset can also be applied to the way we think about our future career planning.

Fixed mindset

Approaching career planning from a fixed mindset can cause people to become inflexible and focus too narrowly on future options. This means that once you find something you are interested in, you stop considering other options and focus all of your attention on one specific pathway. This often leads to disappointment and frustration if things don't work out as planned, because the reality is that you can't predict the future! It can also mean that you could miss out on discovering something that might suit you better because you aren't open to new possibilities or alternative ideas.

For example, if you are operating from the perspective of a fixed mindset, you may think that there is one perfect course or job that is the ideal match for you, and the secret to your future happiness is working out what that specific course or job is. You can get stuck thinking too far into the future and then find it hard to take the first step in your career planning. It might feel like you need to know exactly what job you want and exactly what your career is going to look like before you can decide on the 'right' course.

The problem with this type of thinking is that it is difficult to understand a career (or even a course) until you are in it, engaging in the learning and training, and experiencing it for yourself. This means that it is difficult to know if you are going to like something until you have actually tried it out for yourself. Another issue is that courses take time to complete. Your perfect job may exist now, but will it still exist as it currently looks in three, four, five or even 10 years when you have finished studying and are ready to enter the workforce?

Growth mindset

People who adopt a growth mindset are more willing to embrace uncertainty, focusing on being curious and trying out new things instead of fixating on one specific outcome. You might have a few different courses or jobs that you are interested in and you are excited by the opportunity to explore these options by doing things like work experience, participating in industry immersions, listening to industry experts or even going to TAFE or university open days and information sessions.

You know that the worst thing that could happen is that you find out more information about a course or job and this helps you to realise that you don't actually like it, or it isn't what you thought it would be. You also acknowledge that this is OK because it means that you can cross that possibility off your list and investigate something else instead. It might be a similar course or job, or a complete change in direction.

People who have a growth mindset don't give up if things don't work out as planned; instead, they use the skills and experiences that they have gained to look for new opportunities and new avenues to explore.

CHAPTER 5

Setting goals for future success

Now you have a clearer understanding of who you are and the factors that influence how you think about your world, it is time to start exploring future possibilities. A key to this involves creating goals.

Why is goal setting important?

Goal setting provides you with focus and a purpose. It helps you to define, articulate and plan for your future. Goal setting can help you to create new behaviours, gain new skills or experiences and can make you feel more motivated to take action. As you progress towards your goals, you gain a sense of accomplishment and fulfilment. This can be true even if you don't reach the initial goal! Often, the process of working towards the goal can be as fulfilling as reaching the goal itself.

Not all goals are created equal!

Once you are clear about what you want to achieve, you can start setting goals. There are two main types of goals that can help you with career planning. These are outcome goals and process goals.

Outcome goals

Outcome goals focus on the end result (hence the name!). These are big-picture, long-term goals. Successfully achieving outcome goals can sometimes be out of your control as they may be impacted by external or independent factors. If you don't reach your desired outcome goal, it doesn't mean you have failed!

An example of an outcome goal might be to achieve a specific Australian Tertiary Admission Rank (ATAR) or gain entry to a specific course at university. Remember that outcome goals can be impacted by external factors. You may work hard all year, perform well on all of your assessments, but not get the exact ATAR that you desire. This is because ATAR calculation is based on a range of factors, not just your individual performance. Likewise, successful admission into a university course can depend on your ATAR, the number of applicants (and how you performed in comparison) and the number of places available on the course.

Process goals

Process goals focus on the steps or actions that can help you reach your desired outcome or end result. Process goals tend to be concrete, short term and potentially more achievable.

When thinking about process goals, you need to ask yourself:

- What do I need to do to get to where I want to be?
- What am I willing to change or sacrifice to get there?

An example of a process goal might be to spend a specific number of hours studying each week, attending a specific number of university information events, or completing work experience or volunteering in a field of interest. You have more control over the outcome of these types of goals. Having clearly defined process goals is also shown to help focus your attention, increase your levels of motivation and reduce anxiety.

Four steps to achieving your goals

It is likely that you have been asked to set some goals before. At the start of most school years or after you have received feedback on an assessment task, it is common to be asked to write down or think about how you would like to improve or do things differently in the future. How many of these goals have you actually followed through on? Have you even given these goals a second thought, or is the piece of paper that you wrote them on still crumpled up in the bottom of your bag or locker?

Meaningful goal setting is not a 'set and forget' process. You won't start achieving your goals just because you identified them.

The next chapter provides you with a four-step process to help you go from a dream to reality!

CHAPTER 6

Dream it and make it visual

Step 1: Dream it!

> "Without leaps of imagination or dreaming, we lose the excitement of possibilities. Dreaming, after all, is a form of planning."
> – Gloria Steinem

The first step in successful goal setting involves brainstorming. In the fields of design and marketing, this stage is called ideation and, as the name suggests, this is the ideas phase. Brainstorming involves creativity, imagination and the ability to dream big in order to generate as many ideas or leads as possible. This means looking at your future options from all different angles and perspectives and considering all possibilities, even the crazy or far-fetched ones.

Vision boards

At this stage it can be helpful to start off with a vision board that allows you to identify and visualise the things that you would like to achieve. Don't be limited by negative automatic thoughts. Remember that you are the main character in your story, so place yourself at the centre of your vision board. Surround yourself by the things that you enjoy, the things that you are passionate about, the things that you value and that motivate you. Then, start to consider what you are curious about or what you want to explore further. What do you want to learn or experience? What do you aspire to achieve, be or do? It's time to push yourself outside of your comfort zone and ask yourself: "What if?"

Make your vision board as visual as possible by including images, inspirational photos and symbols, not just words. Let your imagination run wild! The exciting thing about the dreaming stage is that there are no boundaries or limits. Some of the ideas and possibilities that you identify may be unrealistic for you to achieve right now (or maybe ever), but there could be a version of that dream that is achievable.

For example, you may want to become the coach of an elite sports team. While this dream may be difficult to achieve (but not impossible – these coaches do exist!), you may instead focus on developing and enhancing your coaching skills by volunteering at local sporting teams and investigating education and training that will allow you to develop your understanding of elite sport, leadership and coaching skills.

Take action!

Create a brainstorm or vision board that considers the following:

- What do you want your life to look like in one year?
  Two years?
  Five years?
- Where do you want to be?
- What do you want to see, think, feel, be doing?

Step 2: Make it visible

Once you have a vision of what your future might look like and all of the possibilities that could exist, you need to begin to define your career problem. What are you trying to achieve? What questions do you want answered? What do you want to learn or achieve? What steps do you need to take to move you from where you are right now to where you want to be in the future?

Take action!

What are your career-planning priorities right now?
- Is it deciding on subjects to pick in Years 11 and 12?
- Is it thinking about what you might like to do or study when you finish high school?
- Do you want to know more about different career options and pathways?

Select the outcome goal you want to focus on and state your goal in a sentence. For example, "In two years I want to be starting university, studying a degree in…" or "In one year I want to be participating in a gap year program in Europe".

Next, identify the steps or actions that need to be taken to move you towards your desired outcome.

Step 3: SMART goals

Turn your steps into actionable process goals using the SMART approach. SMART goals are an effective way of creating goals that are more likely to actually be achieved. To make a SMART goal, it must be:

Specific: Be very clear about what it is that you want to achieve. Think carefully about the what, where, when and how.

Measurable: Quantify what you want to achieve. Focusing on the numbers makes it easier to track your progress.

Achievable: Set a goal that challenges you but is still something that you can realistically achieve.

Relevant: Make sure your goal is aligned with the direction that you want to head in. Your goal must align with dreams and values, and help you progress towards your outcome goal.

Timebound: It may be helpful to set a timeframe or deadline for your goal to keep you motivated and on task.

Chase goals

An example of a SMART goal:

> *By the end of August this year, I want to have visited three universities that offer degrees in Sport and Exercise Science. I want to ask questions about prerequisites and unit offerings, and find out more about the facilities and industry-based learning opportunities.*

It is also important to take some time to think about and reflect on your process goals once you have identified them. What challenges or barriers may limit your ability to achieve these goals? Are these challenges internal or external?

Make a deal with yourself: have you ever heard of the game Kiss, Marry, Avoid? You can apply this concept to your goal setting! What are you willing to change, commit to or sacrifice to avoid the challenges and barriers and increase your chances of success?

Step 4: Write it down

Writing down your goals and making them visible helps you to get the ideas out of your head and onto paper. It allows you to organise your thoughts and helps you to clear your mind. Writing down your goals makes them more tangible!

Having a clear list of goals displayed in a visible location also means that you are able to keep on track more easily and be more accountable. Because your goals will remain in focus, you may be more likely to notice when relevant opportunities arise and therefore be better prepared to take advantage of them.

A 2015 study by psychologist Gail Matthews found that when people wrote their goals down, they were 33% more successful in achieving them than those who formulated outcomes in their heads.

A study by the Harvard Business school also found that 10 years after graduating the MBA, the 3% of graduates who had written goals and a plan for action ended up earning up to 10 times more than the remaining 97% of graduates.

Take action!

- Create a visual list of your goals (both the short-term process goals and the long-term outcome goal/s).
- Identify any challenges and barriers as well as the strategies that you have identified to overcome them.

You may want to create a vision board-style goal list or a more traditional written list with checkboxes so you can keep track of your progress. Display your goals in a place that you see/visit regularly. This could be on the wall in your bedroom, or as the background on your phone or laptop.

CHAPTER 7

Take your dream for a test drive!

"There's no such thing as a creative type… creativity is a verb. A very time-consuming verb. It's about taking an idea in your head, and transforming that idea into something real. And that's always going to be a long and difficult process. If you're doing it right, it's going to feel like work."

– Milton Glaser

The only way to know whether or not your dream can become reality is if you test it out. While brainstorming is an essential stage of career planning, your journey must not stop there! Being curious about your future options involves both planning and doing.

There is also no purpose in setting goals for yourself if you aren't going to do anything about them. In fact, spending too much time thinking about your future choices rather than taking action can lead to two major issues:

1. You can become overwhelmed or caught up in choice paralysis. This happens when you have too many ideas or options to pick from. Instead of being able to confidently make a decision, you feel overwhelmed and confused, and then find it difficult to settle on just one option because you fear making the wrong choice or missing out on a better option. It's kind of like trying to pick a TV show to watch on a streaming service. Often you spend more time searching for something to watch than actually watching it!

2. If you spend all of your time dreaming about a future career rather than actually testing it out, you might be inclined to 'fill in the gaps' of your understanding of that career with your own ideas rather than actual facts. This romanticised version of the career can lead to unrealistic goals or expectations and future disappointment. This is because the reality of the job might be very different to what you imagined it would be like.

Obviously, taking action to explore your career goals is essential. Taking action involves gathering information and gaining new experiences. This in turn helps you to test out your dreams and see whether or not they are viable.

Taking action does not have to involve huge tasks. It could involve organising work experience, going to a university open day, listening to a career talk or participating in an industry excursion. The main purpose is to explore, learn and gather as much information as possible.

Work experience and industry immersion

There are reasons why work experience and industry immersion are so important.

Work experience

Work experience is a formal arrangement that allows you to visit a workplace for a set period of time (usually a week or two) and learn about the different jobs that exist within that workplace.

Work experience normally involves job shadowing. You may be placed with one supervisor during your entire placement or have the opportunity to work across a range of different areas and alongside different supervisors. The purpose is not for you to actually work, but to learn about the workplace and the different roles required to allow that workplace to function.

Industry immersion

Similar to work experience is industry immersion. This type of experience usually involves a one-off visit, normally in a small group, where you are offered a tour or a 'behind-the-scenes' look at a specific business or organisation. There may also be the opportunity to hear from key staff who discuss their role and day-to-day work tasks. This type of experience is generally organised through your school and may be linked to a specific subject area.

The benefits of experience

Both work experience and industry immersion are beneficial from the perspective of career exploration and development because they help you gain an insight into what things are actually like within a specific industry or workplace, not what you imagine them to be. These experiences can help you to gain a clearer understanding of the day-to-day realities of the industry, workplace culture and expectations, as well as the specific type of work undertaken and the diverse range of career opportunities available. This may help you to clarify your career goals and job preferences, and gain a clearer understanding of whether or not a particular career path actually aligns with your interests and goals.

Connecting with people who already work within the industry you are interested in also allows for networking opportunities. By connecting with current employees, potential mentors and industry professionals, you are beginning to develop connections that can open doors to future opportunities, such as job referrals, as well as valuable sources of advice and career support.

Learn more about your study options

Another way of testing out your career dreams relates to exploring your education options. Just like a job, you can often 'fall in love' with the idea of a particular course without actually understanding much about the course itself.

Most TAFEs and universities offer a range of programs, activities and events designed to help you gain an insight into their course offerings. This could include interactive workshops, shadowing current students, campus tours and the opportunity to participate in lectures. These events and activities give you the chance to ask questions, explore unit offerings, hear about opportunities for overseas travel and the chance to participate in clubs and teams. They also help you to find out about extra opportunities such as work placements, internships and project-based learning, as well as graduate career outcomes – all of the important stuff that is going to help you to make good career decisions about your future!

The difference between TAFE and university

There tends to be a lot of confusion about the difference between TAFE and university. Both options allow you to gain skills, knowledge, experience and qualifications that will help you achieve your career goals. The biggest differences relate to the type of qualifications on offer and the style of teaching.

TAFE

TAFE is designed to make you industry ready. It provides you with the skills and knowledge that employers and industry need, and it often includes a compulsory number of work placement hours or 'on-the-job' learning. TAFE courses tend to be shorter (ranging from a couple of months to up to two years) and are more focused on the practical skills and knowledge required in the workplace. The focus of assessment is on the demonstration of your skills or ability to complete a task correctly.

TAFE can provide a great introduction to an industry and offer a 'low-risk' opportunity to explore post-school options. If you aren't 100% sure about a career pathway, you may like to complete a certificate course at TAFE to try it out. If you like it, you can build on your qualifications by progressing through to a diploma or advanced diploma; or if you really like it, you may want to move on to a related degree course at university. If you don't like it, you have only invested a small amount of time, but gained some employment skills and new knowledge. You can also cross that career option off your list!

In many ways, TAFE courses focus more on the 'what' and 'how' of a job: What do I need to know? What do I need to be able to do? How do I do it? Examples of TAFE courses could include certificates or diplomas in a range of areas, such as hospitality, trades, health and community services, business and information technology.

University

While TAFE tends to teach the 'what' and 'how', university encourages you to think about the 'why'. University is designed to build on your knowledge and understanding by focusing on theory, research and developments in our understanding of a specific topic or area of study over time. University courses tend to be longer (three to four years), and while the focus of assessment varies depending on the subject area, it can include essays, research projects, case studies and examinations.

Combining post-school options

The good news is that TAFE and university are not mutually exclusive – that is, you don't have to pick one option and stick with it forever! Many people start off studying at TAFE because they want an introduction to an industry and the basic skills to start working within that industry sooner rather than later. Once they have more experience, they may want to upgrade their qualification or gain more advanced skills by completing further training and education at either TAFE or university.

An example might be someone who initially completes a carpentry apprenticeship. After working in the building and construction industry for a few years and gaining more experience and knowledge, a carpenter might want to become a building inspector by completing an additional qualification at TAFE. Alternatively, they may want to use their skills, knowledge and experience to become a project manager by gaining an additional qualification at university.

Someone who has initially completed a university degree may also go on to complete a TAFE course to fill in gaps in their knowledge or gain more practical skills. For example, a person who completed a business degree may want to gain specialist or practical skills in digital media advertising or website development through a certificate or diploma course at TAFE.

The most important thing to keep in mind when thinking about post-school pathways is that one option is not better than the other. Rather, one option may be better suited to you at a particular point in time when you consider your learning needs and your desired outcome. Find the option that is going to serve you best in the next step of your education and career journey!

CHAPTER 8

Top tips and advice when considering study options

Make sure your study pathway is aligned with your career goals!

Perhaps the most important first step when considering your study options is to actually review your potential career options. Some jobs require a specific qualification in order to gain professional accreditation or membership within the industry. This includes jobs such as an accountant, architect or engineer. Other jobs such as electrician, plumber or hairdresser require the completion of an apprenticeship, which combines work with study and may take three to four years to complete.

Will you need a qualification?

If you have a specific career goal in mind, then you need to make sure that you are completing the correct qualification. If you aren't sure if the job you are interested in requires a specific qualification, do some research. Most jobs will have a professional association website that has a page dedicated to explaining what you need to do to work in that industry.

Not all jobs require a specific qualification. Some require a certain level of education, training or experience but are flexible with what that looks like. If you are interested in an industry but aren't sure exactly what job you want to pursue yet, a good starting point is to have a look on a job search website. Select the industry area you are interested in (it might be business, professional services, construction) and then explore the different jobs that are currently advertised. This is useful for two reasons:

1. It gives you an insight into the types of jobs available within the industry.

2. It helps you to understand what the labour market looks like. This allows you to gain an awareness of salary expectations, the required levels of education and training, and the number of jobs available in your area.

All of this information can help you make informed decisions about your future career goals.

Focus on *what* you want to study, not *where* you want to study

Sometimes it can be easy to get caught up in the idea of going to university, even when the area that you want to study isn't offered at a university level. In fact, you may find that TAFE offers a more specific course that better meets your needs and interests. An example of this could include something like real estate, landscaping or community services.

Likewise, you might become obsessed with the reputation of a specific university or education provider, even though that university or education provider doesn't actually offer the course that you want to study. Remember, there is no point in going to a specific university just to say that you went there if it doesn't actually offer the course you want or need to study! An example of this is a university that only offers general degrees like Arts, Business and Science, when you have your heart set on a specialised degree like Nursing, Teaching or Law. You may still be able to achieve your career goal by undertaking postgraduate or further study, but it will probably take longer and cost a lot more money.

Spend some time carefully considering the following questions: What is your ultimate aim? To go to university? To go to a specific university? Or to study a course that is aligned with your needs and interests and one that will allow you to move towards your career goals? Work out what your priority is and pursue it!

Get stuck into the nitty-gritty

It may not come as a surprise, but you need to invest as much time into investigating course options as you do investigating career options. Trying to navigate your post-school study paths can be confusing. Often, different providers offer the same courses and the same providers offer different courses that kind of look and sound the same!

You need to look beyond the course title and consider what you will actually be studying. If you are thinking about going to university, you might come across words like 'majors', 'minors' and 'core subjects'. Majors and minors are basically the things you want to specialise in. Core subjects are the compulsory subjects that everyone must complete. These are usually foundational knowledge-type subjects or ones that are required for professional accreditation.

For example, if you are studying a Bachelor of Business, you may like to complete a major in Human Resource Management and a minor in Entrepreneurial Business Practice. The course rules will tell you how many units in a particular area you need to complete in order for that area to 'count' as a major or a minor. Core units could include subjects like Introduction to Business Ethics or Professional Practice for the Business Environment. These subjects are relevant to all students studying the degree, no matter what they decide to major in.

Most of the time, the university has already mapped out the subjects linked to each major and/or minor and they will clearly identify which subjects are core units, so all you have to do is pick the area you want to specialise in and enrol in those subjects.

Something to keep in mind is that while you may be able to study a course with the same title at different places, the structure of the course, the way that the course is taught and the things that you can study within the course may look very different, and this is why research is so important!

What will set you apart from everyone else?

While most TAFE courses have a strong employability focus embedded within the program, a common mistake that many university students make is waiting until the end of their degree to start building their employability skills and experiences. A better approach is to think about how you can start making yourself attractive to a potential employer from day one. There are two major benefits to this approach:

1. Building your employability skills and experiences early means that you have plenty of time to explore different options and gain lots of different experiences – you aren't rushing at the end of your course to cram things in!

2. It gives you time to reassess your goals and make changes if needed. For example, if you are studying communications, you may volunteer one day a week at your local community radio station. During this time, you realise that broadcasting is different to what you thought it would be like and you are actually more interested in digital media. If you discover this early on in your course, you should have time to change majors with little to no disruption.

Making connections

Building your employability skills and experiences involves connecting with industry and employers. It involves developing the skills that are required by employees within your chosen industry and often means applying the knowledge that you learn through your course to real-life situations. This can be achieved through activities such as volunteering, work placements and internships, industry-based projects and mentoring opportunities.

The graduate employment market can be tough! Each year, thousands of students are finishing their courses with the same qualification and competing for the same jobs. Throughout your course, you need to actively be thinking about and securing opportunities that will set you apart from all the other students that are studying the same thing as you.

Having a resume that showcases industry engagement throughout your course is an effective way to do this. Make sure that when you are researching your course options, you look for programs that focus on developing your employability skills and ones that allow you to engage in industry-based experiences.

CHAPTER 9

Start building your skills and experience now!

Your career journey starts today

Up until this point, we have spoken a lot about your career future. But the reality is, you can start making progress on your career today.

There are two main ways that you can achieve this:

1. Developing employability skills through activities at school
2. Getting a part-time or casual job

When it comes to applying for your first job, a lot of young people get stuck because they don't think they have much to include on a resume. After all, how can you talk about your work-related skills if you haven't started work yet? But the truth is you probably already have a range of useful skills and experiences that make you work-ready, before you have secured your first job.

Developing employability skills

Employability skills like communication, teamwork, problem-solving and time management are not just developed in a work setting. These are skills that you are most likely already practising every day at school.

In class

You might be developing these skills through the activities that you do within the classroom or through the assessment tasks that you complete. Every day at school is an opportunity to practise and develop these skills. For example, you may be asked to complete a group research task and presentation for class. By actively participating in this task, you are learning to work collaboratively with others, plan ahead and manage your time effectively, and communicate with your peers. These experiences are all great preparation for the workplace.

Outside class

You can also enhance your employability skills and gain valuable experiences by participating in extracurricular activities such as camps and sports, and through leadership programs or social justice activities. You can also develop these skills and experiences through activities that you do outside of school, by participating in different hobbies and getting involved in community groups and volunteering. Participating in activities outside of the classroom shows your willingness to give things a go and be pushed outside your comfort zone. It can also help you learn to balance your time and commitments, and allow you to work closely with people you may not normally work with.

For example, you may volunteer once a week at your local club's junior footy sessions, helping to run clinics and mini games for the under 7s. As part of this, you organise the equipment, set up the activities and offer help and advice to the children on your team. Through this experience, you are developing skills such as leadership, communication and organisation. All of these skills are valuable when you are looking for your first (or second) job. So, when it's time to sit down and write your resume, think broadly and creatively about all of the things that you have been involved in both inside and outside of the classroom, and the variety of skills that you have been developing.

Participation

What if you haven't been involved in much? Change that! Find something you are interested in and get involved. Developing employability skills isn't restricted to participation in sport. Your school might offer a range of clubs or groups that you can get involved with, based on a variety of interests, such as environment and sustainability, gaming or cultural groups.

Outside of school, local libraries and community organisations will also often offer a range of activities and groups that you can participate in. It can be a little scary to push outside your comfort zone, engage in new experiences and meet new people. By focusing on something that you are already interested in, you can enhance your existing passion and interests, and develop new ones. You can also meet people who share your interests and passions. The confidence and independence that you can gain through these types of experiences are also helpful when you do secure your first job.

Getting a part-time or casual job

There are many benefits to getting your first part-time or casual job. Making money and meeting new people are the most common reasons that young people want to start working, but research tells us that there are long-term benefits for your career, too.

According to longitudinal studies (that is research that checks in with a participant at different points over a number of years or different stages of their life), young people who combine work with study are better off long term. These benefits include higher earnings, fewer periods of unemployment and greater career satisfaction. Interestingly, though, the number of hours that a person works is important, with too many hours being associated with poorer academic performance at school.

Things to consider

Managing work and school is definitely a juggling act, but this juggling act is teaching you how to manage your time and competing tasks, prioritise and problem-solve. These are essential skills for future employment. Before you start looking for a job, think carefully about the number of hours that you have available to work, taking into account other responsibilities and commitments, such as homework, assignments, sport and other hobbies.

It is also important to think about the jobs that may be available in your area and how you will get to work. Will you be relying on your parents to drive you or is there public transport available? What opportunities for work exist outside of school hours?

Potential employers

The most common industries that employ young people are hospitality and food services, retail and recreational services, so start to think about potential employers in your local area. You may like to make a list of restaurants, cafés, fast-food businesses, supermarkets and other retail and recreational outlets that are open in the evenings or on the weekends. If you play sport, there may also be opportunities to do coaching or umpiring for junior teams, so ask around at your local club.

Resumes and cover letters

Before you can apply for a job, you will need a resume and a cover letter.

Resumes

A resume is a snapshot of your education and employment history. It should include information such as your skills, experiences and major achievements, as well as personal information like your name, where you go to school and what you are studying.

Your resume doesn't need to be long. You might find that your first resume is only one page in length. This is OK! As long as the information is relevant and it showcases your qualities to a potential employer, the exact length doesn't matter. Your resume will naturally get longer over time as you gather new experiences and build new skills.

Cover letters

A cover letter is a quick way to 'talk' directly to the employer, introducing yourself, highlighting your top skills and explaining why you are applying for work. Again, a cover letter should be short and to the point – one page is generally the expected length.

Keep them updated

While it is a good idea to have a standard resume and cover letter on file, it is important to make sure that you are adjusting and reviewing these documents every time you apply for a new job. It is also really important to tailor these documents in response to the job that you are applying for. You can do this by identifying the key skills and experiences that the employer is looking for (this information is usually in the job ad) and highlighting how you meet these requirements by showcasing these skills and experiences in your resume and cover letter.

Looking for work

The next step is to find out how potential employers recruit staff and whether or not they are currently hiring. Some major retailers or larger companies may require you to apply online via their website. They may even encourage you to register for job alerts if they aren't currently hiring. Smaller businesses may advertise opportunities in-store, so keep an eye out for advertising in store windows next time you are out shopping, going out for dinner or going to the movies.

Another option is to do some 'cold calling'. Cold calling involves approaching an employer that is not currently hiring and enquiring about job opportunities, providing them with your resume. It can show confidence and a willingness to be proactive. This approach works better for small businesses that have greater flexibility when hiring.

Preparing for an interview

If an employer likes what they see in your resume and cover letter, you may be asked to come in for a job interview. An interview may be one to one (for example, you and the employer) or involve a small group of applicants (this often happens when an employer needs to recruit a large number of staff at the same time, like for busy Christmas periods or when a business is first opening).

Interviews can be face to face, online or even over the phone. Different businesses will run interviews in different ways. Some may take a more formal approach by asking you a series of questions designed to assess your experience, skills and suitability to the role. Others will just want to have an informal chat with you, to see if you are a good 'fit' for the business.

Preparation is key

Whether the interview is formal or informal, it is always a good idea to make sure that you feel prepared. You can do this by revisiting the job ad and thinking about the qualities, skills and experience the employer is looking for. For example, employers are often looking for staff who can work independently and part of a team if required, people who are friendly and who can communicate well, problem-solve and manage their time effectively. They may also seek out staff who can show initiative, work well under pressure and manage conflict if it arises.

Interview questions

Knowing what an employer is looking for helps you to work out the types of questions that they may ask you in an interview.

Below are some commonly asked interview questions that might help get you started:

> *Can you tell me about yourself?*
>
> *What personal qualities or attributes do you think you could bring to this role?*
>
> *Tell me about a time when you worked as part of a team. What were the challenges? How did you overcome these challenges?*
>
> *Imagine you are at work and you are confronted by an angry customer. How would you respond?*
>
> *Have you ever been given an instruction or asked to perform a task that you didn't understand? How did you approach this situation? What steps did you take to find out more information?*

Use these practice questions as a starting point to begin thinking about real-life examples that you could use. You may like to start by writing down responses to these questions and then by practising in front of a mirror. Once you are feeling more confident, ask a friend or family member to interview you.

Practice makes PROGRESS

On the day of the interview

You will most likely be feeling a little nervous on the day of your interview. Keep in mind that the more interviews that you attend, the easier they will get.

Don't be late

Being organised can also help make things a little bit easier. Before the day of your interview, get familiar with the interview location, how you are going to get there and how long it will take. You should aim to arrive around 20 minutes early just in case you (or your parents) struggle to find a car park or traffic is an issue. Sometimes finding the exact location of the interview can be tricky, so having some extra time means that you aren't getting stressed about also running late. Try to avoid making an interview straight after school. School traffic is unpredictable, and you may feel rushed to get changed and get to the interview if you don't leave yourself enough time.

Dress to impress – but don't overdo it

It is important to think about your appearance prior to the interview. Again, you need to think about the workplace that you are applying to work in. How do existing employees present themselves? If you are applying for a role as a food and beverage attendant at a high-end hospitality venue, the chances are that the employer is looking for staff who are neat, tidy and well-presented. For this type of interview, dress on the conservative side: plain black pants or a skirt and a button-up shirt create a good impression, and make sure that your hair is neat and tidy. Avoid excessive make-up or jewellery.

However, some workplace environments encourage creativity and personality, and it is OK to show this in an interview, too. For example, if you are interviewing for a position at a fashion retailer, it is a good idea to wear something that highlights your interest in fashion; or if you are interviewing for a job at a bookshop, wearing your Gryffindor socks creates a talking point during the interview.

First impressions

Another good approach to take is to imagine that your interview has started as soon as you arrive at the interview venue. Since you probably don't know who is interviewing you, be friendly and polite to everyone you meet. This helps to create a positive impression with all staff. Make sure your phone is on silent and keep it out of view in your pocket or bag, even if you are asked to wait. This will help you avoid getting distracted prior to your interview and will help make you look more professional.

Try to relax

When you are in the interview, try to remember that the people asking the questions are human, too! They will understand that you are probably nervous. Don't hesitate to accept a glass of water if it is offered, or ask them to repeat a question or explain a question further if you don't understand or need to think about your response for a moment.

At the end of the interview, you might be asked if you have any questions. You may like to have a question or two prepared to ask, or something might have popped up during the interview that you would like to clarify or ask more about. This is your chance to do so. But don't worry if you don't have a question to ask. Some interviewers do such a good job that they tell you everything that you need to know.

After the interview

It might take a couple of days for you to hear anything back after your interview. Try to be patient. If it gets to a week and you haven't had a response, it is a good idea to call and find out how your application is progressing.

What happens if I'm unsuccessful?

It might take a couple of interviews before you secure a job. Don't give up! There can be lots of reasons why you aren't offered a position, especially when you are at the start of your career journey. Spend some time reflecting on the interview questions and your responses to them. Could you have added more detail or included a more specific example? Is there a way that you could have answered with more confidence or highlighted your skills and knowledge in a better way?

Just because you didn't get the job, it doesn't mean that you didn't do the right thing or that you didn't answer the questions well enough. It may have come down to other factors, such as your fit with the company or your availability. While reflection is important, try not to get stuck on what did or didn't happen. Treat it as a learning experience and keep searching.

What happens if I'm successful?

Congratulations! Getting your first (or second, or tenth) job can be very exciting. Before you start, make sure that you know a few things.

Type of employment

One of the first things to check is whether you are being employed as a casual or part-time staff member (there is a difference!). The hours that a casual staff member works can vary from week to week. Some weeks you might get two or three shifts (maybe even more if it is school holidays), and other weeks you might only get one shift. Casuals normally get paid at a higher rate per hour because they don't get other benefits like a set roster, sick pay or holiday pay. Part-time staff have set hours that they work each week. These do not vary from week to week unless you agree to a specific change in your roster. Part-time staff accrue holiday pay and have access to personal leave (pay for when you are sick or unable to attend your normal shift).

Wages

It is also really important that you have a clear understanding of how much you will be paid. Most workplaces will be part of an industry-based award, which outlines pay and other entitlements such as breaks, allowances and penalty rates. Make sure that you know which award applies to your workplace (if you aren't provided with a copy when you start, you can access them online), and if you are ever in doubt, check it out!

Another useful source of information is your payslip. All employees are required to receive a payslip. This should include details of the hours you have worked, how much you have earned (both during that pay period and for the financial year) and other details, such as the amount being paid to your superannuation fund (yes, you need one even if you are a teenager and you won't be retiring for many, many years!) and the amount you have paid in tax.

Ironing out uncertainties

One of the biggest issues faced by young workers is that they don't know how to respond to difficult situations or how to ask when they don't know something. This can have serious consequences. Unfortunately, it can mean that you aren't paid correctly or that you miss out on things that you are entitled to, such as breaks. It can also mean that you are put in situations that are unsafe.

If at any moment when you start work you are uncertain about something, you don't know what to do or you don't feel safe, you must speak up. Talk to someone you trust at work, or tell your parents or a careers teacher at school. Find out what your rights are and work out how to bring this up with your employer so that things can be resolved before they get worse. Earning money and developing skills are great, but your safety and wellbeing are more important.

CHAPTER 10

Reflect, evaluate and readjust

Your career journey will most likely not be linear. It is highly unlikely that you will pick subjects for senior school, identify a career you want to pursue and complete the necessary education or training pathway, and go directly into a job that you will stay in for the rest of your working life.

It can be helpful to imagine that you are the captain of a boat. You have mapped out your journey and set sail. Some days may be smooth sailing and you make excellent progress towards your desired destination. Other days, you may encounter stormy weather that knocks you off course and causes you to redirect or change course entirely. Career planning is very similar.

Be adaptable

Life is full of surprises, disappointments, setbacks and new opportunities. Things are changing all the time. The most important thing is to be open to change, be flexible and curious, and demonstrate willingness to learn and grow. At every point in your career journey, take time to pause, reflect, evaluate and readjust if necessary.

For example, once you have completed work experience or an industry-immersion activity, you may want to consider the following:

Was the work environment what I was expecting?

What new information did I learn about the specific jobs?

Were my expectations or beliefs confirmed or challenged?

Did this experience improve my understanding of the industry and the related occupations?

Likewise, maybe you had the opportunity to visit a TAFE or university to learn more about course options. Afterwards, it is worth thinking about whether the course was aligned with your study or career goals, and you may want to consider the following:

Did the units on offer interest you?

Did the mode of study suit your learning style?

Did the course get you excited about the next step in your career journey?

If you are answering "no" to these questions, it might be time to revisit your goals and make some changes. Remember, career planning is not a one-time process. It is something that you will do over and over again throughout your career life. The key to success lies in the mindset or approach that you adopt.

The key to success

A successful career mindset is one that:

- Embraces change, is curious about new possibilities and is willing to experiment and try things out
- Is reflective and able to readjust to overcome setbacks and challenges, reframe problems, and seek out help and advice

Every step you take towards achieving your goals is helping you to learn and grow, write and rewrite your career narrative. You are gathering information that is helping you get to the next step in your career journey.

Finally, do not forget that there is never one specific career pathway or ideal job for you. There is an unlimited number of potential pathways and opportunities that could bring you happiness and success. Your goal should be to find the one that most suits you at the stage of your life you are in right now. That may change in the future as you gather new information about yourself, your industry and the world of work in general. And this is OK! Once you learn the process of career planning, you can continue to use those skills again and again throughout your life.

Good luck!

Milton Keynes UK
Ingram Content Group UK Ltd.
UKHW020640270524
443094UK00001B/1